D0886574

GHOSTWOOD

GHOSTWOOD

POEMS BY STAR BLACK

MELVILLE HOUSE
HOBOKEN, NEW JERSEY

©2003 Star Black

Melville House Publishing
P.O. Box 3278
Hoboken, NJ 07030

Series editors: Valerie Merians and Dennis Loy Johnson
Design and photography: David Konopka

ISBN: 0-9718659-2-2

First Edition April 2003

                    Library of Congress Cataloging-in-Publication Data

Black, Star.
    Ghostwood / Star Black.– 1st ed.
        p. cm.
    ISBN 0-9718659-2-2 (hardcover)
    1. Sonnets, American. I. Title.
    PS3552.L34134G48 2003
    811'.54--dc21

                                                2003000163

ACKNOWLEDGEMENTS

Grateful acknowledgement is made to the following publications in which these poems first appeared:

"Edge of Spring" in *Barrow Street*; "Auto-Autumn," in *Ploughshares;* "Atonement," "Skyscapers" and "Perfect Weather" in *110 Stories: New York Writers After September 11*, edited by Elrich Baer (New York University Press); "Asylum" and "Skyscrapers" in *Poetry After 9/11: An Anthology of New York Poets*, edited by Dennis Loy Johnson and Valerie Merians (Melville House Publishing).

The title "There is only sun, sunstrife and sea" is from John Ashbery's poem "The Corrupt Text" in *As Umbrellas Follow Rain* (Qua Books).

Thanks also to Yaddo and the MacDowell Colony, and to David Lehman, Andrea Carter Brown, Grace Schulman, and Bill Knott. "Courting Oriane" is for the painter Darragh Park.

CONTENTS

one
SEPTEMBER ELEVENTH

17 PERFECT WEATHER
19 ASYLUM
20 ATONEMENT
21 SKYSCAPERS

two
LOOSESTRIFE

25 TABLELAND
26 URCHINS
27 NEBULOUS
28 BELOVED
29 MOEBIUS
30 BARTER
31 WEED-DEEP
32 'ORE 'ERE 'ORE
33 COURTING ORIANE
34 LABOR DAY LOST
35 SUNBURST
36 RUFFLED
37 NOIR NIGHTS
38 EDGE OF SPRING
39 RIPOSTE

three
OVERCAST

43 GALLIGASKINS
44 COMFORT
45 SWEET DEMISE
46 FAINT FERVOR
47 THRESHOLD
48 AUTO-AUTUMN
49 REDOLENT WILES
50 MOCK ORANGE
51 NOVEMBER MORE
52 OIL BIRDS
53 GLORY
54 WOMBWARD

four
THE KEYHOLE GARDEN

59 THE KEYHOLE GARDEN
60 FEATHER-FLOWN
61 EASY COMPANY
62 TO A FRIEND WRITING
   A MEMOIR
63 DAYTRIPPING
64 SAVING MONEY
65 BEACH BALM
66 SWEVENS
67 SPRINGWOOD
   ESPOUSAL
68 RIP RAP
69 MESA MISCHIEF
70 RIGHT ON
71 BIRDBATH
72 LAYING LOW
73 "THERE IS ONLY SUN,
   SUNSTRIFE AND SEA"

77 ABOUT THE POET

GHOSTWOOD

Nothing is with me now but a sound,
    A heart's rhythm, a sense of stars
Leisurely walking around, and both
    Talk in a language of motion
I can measure but not read ...

W.H. Auden

one **SEPTEMBER ELEVENTH**

PERFECT WEATHER

I

The sky was so clear, the morning beautiful,
the weather fair, neither hot nor cool, the tower
aflame far down the avenue, a white smokestack
seen at eye-level, a huge, multi-alarm fire

firefighters attend to, and then, like the descent
of chalk on a blackboard behind all that is remembered,
behind the mind, behind the apprehended,
a sight without reference, the building

ended. The next burned as a thick candle
and then there was no candle and everyone was
quiet and the traffic ended and the tunnels

closed and the trains stopped and the phones
were busy and the children showed up, finally, finally,
and there was no snow like long ago. No beautiful snow.

II

So many walked and walked and did not talk.
All dressed for the office. There were no offices.
All dressed for construction. There was no construction.
The bus drivers drove until there were no buses.

Those who talked could not say much. All talk
was on television. Nothing was rushed; midtown
was quieted by a formal mutation between what will be
and what was. What was was a cafe,

what was was clear water, what was
was a supermarket with so many shoppers,
the cashiers as busy as the cashiers one remembers,
and the clarity of air; that, too, was familiar,

but now it was all that was there: trapped
desks in a dark cloud rising in the clarity of air.

ASYLUM

In the unmannered madhouse
of the typical mind,
its swinish discontents
and skeetering emotions,

upon its disheveled doss
and rabbly bedspread,
two firebugs
buzz tête-à-tête.

They connect and disconnect
through the dogtooth days.
Pray for them.
They are small and

cannot live inside long.
Open a window.

ATONEMENT

Aged prophets, cradled in Crivelli's gold, on
a heat-waved page replicating quattrocento frescos,
seem shy above the trees' periscopes as if the sky
were an unfamiliar cathedral, and, should they

appear there now, standing between receding
clouds, how gilded their halo, what color their gowns
and what scripted tablet would they hold to admonish
the truculent below, what divine secundum

to calm the skrimble-scramble, to readdress
the compass, its fanning factions for whom Housman
sang so many cold grim songs? The page, an about-face
of opulent faith, seems so removed from

Star Wars and stem cells, nearly out-of-place
were it not for the lushness of detail, the inimitable grace.

SKYSCRAPERS

Night's glass towers, Rapunzel'd by the sun,
still stand at attention when the work's all done
like dragon dogs guarding the Mahayana heavens, or sentries
at the outpost, leaning, nodding. Solariums

of labor, they're useless to the moon, pitched
punctuation without any words. Harbors of security
to paper-clipping functions now rest in darkness
as mute gongs in an infinite forest,

elevators and alarms shut-eyed in silence,
thirteenth floors snuffed. They seem, to tiny slumberers
doorsteps from their lobby, friendly giants

who nuzzle dreams in tiny apartments, as if, tired
from standing, they roll back, as a shoulder onto a pillow,
to let a neighbor know the nightmare's over.

two **LOOSESTRIFE**

TABLELAND

Loosestrife, your negligible plumes, without you
there's little life and less room. You are late summer's
good-night to all unsettling eddies; you uncomplicate festering
complexities. Your bows within a vase quell the gaze

of belles and eunuchs, whiskered snakes, purplish
concealments and whitewashed gates: all disquieting inference,
bad holidays. Do you dream in paragraphs or hulahoops?
Are your mentors geraniums, or fairy-flared hues?

Are you a prodigy like Schubert or a flushed autodidact?
Do you sing for Gretchen in Faust, or are you more private,
a monastic flounce? And what did you do, near azalea
and yew, that brings such solace to the bereft

residues of lingering Fall? Will we ever know,
is it all a thrawned De Soto? Lost sails beyond the view?

URCHINS

The pawns have departed, gone for a swim,
the king broken-hearted, the queen disinterested.
The tight-lipped fiefdom of zooming bishops is tenty
and relieved, as if all the sheaths were missing.

Down by the pool, the sky sate and promising
as a second inning, the romping pawns play Marco Polo
all day long. The castles—grim Zouaves—flare their nostrils
over the too-wide view. The queen, in seas

of ennui, yearns for a chansonnier, someone above
above it all, who is never there and never away. The king
is miserable, as if doom were an endless vestibule
haunted by a double bed. The pawns care less

and less. The sky's bat connects, and it runs home.
Not the pawns, though: no running on Death Row.

NEBULOUS

She was born, she loved someone, someone died,
she was forlorn. Static maps attacked, gagged the scenery.
Shadows in hats panhandled her body. A stylist
slipped her a lemur. She thought it pretty.

Troy swayed, a tantalization below a city,
a kingdom of swamps and silks, a trompe l'oeil of blood,
her body swept up in an orbit of couplets. Two eyes
survived the tumult, the sky's half-tones,

until deciphering seas, embedded in foxglove,
drove through even these, and she became an elision,
a pawn ticket on the carte blanche marl. Yet, there
was always an innocence about it, a wile

in the fore-and-aft itinerary, like an ankle-bracelet
looping a cloud, as if not all were unraveled.

BELOVED

You are many trees within me which is one tree,
your tree, in a thrave of trees, a coventry, which brings
immeasurables, awake in the country, close to me—
a seraph's whistle, an orange egg, a droop

of blue—while tomorrows, quick and common,
depart for more assured armageddons and may their
destinations be well-remembered on the rhomboiding scroll
with greybeard's cherubim semisphered in plundered

gold, streaking go-carts with revelation, but, to return
to your tree that flowers and refills me as the visitor you
loathe and welcome with all the resentments culled
from home, its cozening dejection: yours is

the tree, the faun-cloistered tapestry that nears
the nearest spangle and, in slipknots, slipknots me.

MOEBIUS

The roomette tends to forget the roomette,
as the train's uncolored pantomimes, framed in a roulade
of glass, pass the rockweed rostrums, the grainy
haulms, the rose mallows and peep-show

homes with calamitous windows shaded, the view
a residue, an aquacade without a pool: tombal, outpaced
by the rubbled landscape, its netherworldly pull.

You say the loftiest trees await, unremedial
fronds, bright speculums, their rhythmic obits all
gone into the sequestering beam, the seraphim wing,

not unlike a roomette on slow quaking train
but less dreamy, less innocent, guileless yet not
guileless in the same instant, a wink in a summary,
the trip's forgotten origin its foregone destiny.

BARTER

In Holland, the black tulip grows,
tossing fortunes into severe hollows.

It once was a rhinoceros horn, a tiger's paw,
the brain of a monkey. Everyone knew

the black tulip's rarity. Everyone
wanted a black tulip in their library.

Merchants ordered. They attained.
The tulip strained in these entrancements.

All was well: one black tulip,
two black tulips, in the slippered hall.

The market grew, every tulip
rarified in the black tulip's thrall,

until one baron declined to buy,
and all the tulips in Holland fell to hell.

WEED-DEEP

In a forest appearing as still as a bowling ball
eased between one's hand and a toppling pin, the rain will
not fall, the rain will not begin to begin. Every squirrel
is platonic within the moist cave; there is no

projection, no flickering shade. A sullen amplitude
stills the Graham Greene ish twists within the dark escapade,
as if the plot had gotten away from the pulsing relief
of divine mercy. The air allows one practiced

smile, one smile only, borne as the fleam
of a surgeon entering a chest, thinly. The crickets,
splotched by silence, are leery among the starched leaves.
Their hops are dotty, wrinkling their deliveries,

as dragonflies, quick to the occasion, fornicate rapidly.
Is this the effaced space that binds us, so tightly?

'ORE 'ERE 'ORE

The spoondrift of a lone vowel: the "o" outted
from the memoir leaving the text a screed of reminiscent "e"s,
while, jouncing about, above, on an ontological cloud,
an ornery onanist oo's the outlandish crowd.

Far afield, in furrowed fantasies, flux-flung,
fervent and frisky, furnished with ferret furs and flasks,
flannelled with fleece, the faintly-famished
flee, flushed by feigning flatteries,

affronted by oo-oo's and oo-oo's only. Foo,
there is a tunnel of "of's" somewhere less official
and more overt than this syllabary of fluted fountains
where the on-and-off's convene, sylphly.

There must be, in ogling agos, on the umpteenth storey,
some fond, found force, outted from the office, that's comfy.

COURTING ORIANE

Darragh, in reticence, sketches the ghost of his dog
who, like a cageless parakeet, frets amid the unreformable
apogees, huelessly, as if she will never belong in such high-flung
liberty, among the cloud jackals and wolverines, but longs

for the pillowed couch from where Darragh sees, in
phantoms of spinnakered lines, her limbs, listless as she sleeps,
slipped back to Darragh's side. Is it reverie, or belief, that
keeps the missing so close by? And can the answer

be a revealed in a pen-swept line? Or is the pillowed
hour, hours beyond the clock's shock, a hazed hovering garden
without banishment, with verdant talk, that blooms again,

the gates unlocked, in matrimonies of all love, to remind
those left behind those sent above can intertwine dust with flesh,
clocks with doves, and sleep on a couch that's now and ever was?

LABOR DAY LOST

In elegies of August, lakes are deeply green.
Mists drift above surfaces many drowned suns heat.
Bathers on lunch hour rearrange their knees. Cell phones
and beepers clip the beaches. The mauves are crisp,

no longer indolent, the plastic pails amiss, listless,
their measured heaps of sand tilted, spilt, just below
the docile parking lot where damp towels and burr pricks
once gagged the sheenwater silence. A late day,

enclosed between seasons, phloxes the reticence.
The birches, once imperious, slightly dowse the dull
lusters of sundowns as if to mop the sand, and widows
wonder whom they love, a gnome or a tall man,

two vanishing points on a crinkled photograph, which,
like a leaf, rustles more slowly than it did last week.

SUNBURST

Predeceasing dawn, red leopard in an igloo,
how kindly your creaseless fog surrounds the satinpod
in half-smiles of pallid blue. Too soon the sky's slato is rid of you
and unlamenting, your ice bricks consumed by indigo,

the cloud galleons launched on brisk ventures,
like pages of blank xeroxes, mapping the armada as it moves
away from you, a bloodspot under tissue. Yours is the very
slowest saturation, a milk-whiskered stare that

micromanages the dung beetles, the dewy crinolines
of air, before mizzens rise and sail the jetstreams, saturated
by light. Who can forget you, mute in the lilac avalanche,
mottled limbs pulsing as if in a dance, swished

by bird cries, and whom can you outlast? Or does each
hoisted inception also redden to aphasia, as it enters the past?

RUFFLED

Sunflowers seeds and Sprite grace the shopping list
tonight: Sprite for water in a vase to assure the irises
stay upright in a bay of lemon leaves, and sunflower seeds
for the platoon of chipmunks outside, but what do

you need, a cracked paperweight? An Argus eye?
The whereabouts brim with errands; the pied-a-terre
sky has fallen, trampled by rain, wetting clumsy raspberries
with dew stains, lending avid rocks squirrel fur, plish.

Misinterpretations, like hummingbird wings, fuzz
the phenomenon, making penseurs nervous in quadrilles
of check lists, as if Argus were angry at his bovine

charge and wanted a transfer to another river with
more Daphnes than you could throw at stick at. Oh where
are the keys and where did I park? What blind alley?

NOIR NIGHTS

Red gladiolas margin the dime novels,
saskatooning the hard-boiled details within,
their plumes diminuendos in an hypothesis of stems.
Above the eels, a lamp reddens,

and the man-minutes spin, plinths of history
in hometowns, heading out or heading in,
in a slow crumble of blossoms.

The trees are rough and steady,
and the white moths wild. Gladiolas,
like mythical guardsmen, have a hundred eyes.

They stare, in window-washing crimson,
at the moth-dotted plots where tough men in trucks
of daisies meet and interlock, and all the Schenectadys
step back, in reverence, and all the clocks stop.

EDGE OF SPRING

Rust-colored Aprils, lilac-loose laminations
of laminated blues, rains in fade-outs of sockless
shoes, probing the blue-bells, snowlessly; what is it
you do, in the bird-strewn atrium, that makes

intellectuals weep while schoolgirls bloom?
What fuses the green mayhem that renders paladins
gun shy in mauve, as the silken chrysalis lifts
from the bark continent and lets go? Where

is your love seat? Suspended from which halo?
Mayday, Mayday, is so slow, and you so enwreathingly
subsuming, as if there were so many moderate

vistas to clover, so many wings to re-release,
that the softest nudge is impossible—a cornstalk
affront—to the unrelievingly taut semi-greenness.

RIPOSTE

Mildewed routines face the mirror, dumbly,
in hopes that Daphne will leap from a laurel tree
and dampproof the cowled breeze that signals the acute
absence of leaves, a shoo-in for the sudden

solstice that vanquishes heat; but there is
no nymph, no afterimage, in the hardheaded gaze,
just a ticktocking inches away, a foiled splutter, a dicta
of workdays in a half-time huddle, ready to spring

into play, while, bark-bent and intent, Daphne
repolishes her green nails, lulling in the shushed liberty
of Apollo-free trails, coiled in the sap's hug, furled
and fetching, anticipating winter, its sweet

disengaging release, its snow-quiet effigies
of crunched twigs, its reveling hails and simple sylvan sleep.

three **OVERCAST**

GALLIGASKINS

The sky as flat as the globe has ever been,
the weather a hagborn with a twitch, the nerves
iron-maidens to half-clothed heretics, the black flies
slumped, the mosquitoes hieroglyphs; summer

dodders to a slow close, her habaneras spent,
and saunters among the slow and reliable tombstones
of old friends. Old friends, where have you went?
Is there jelly on your scones? Is there Trivial

Pursuit? What's it like to wear the same old suit?
Is the velvet virile, or is the disco mute? Don't worry
about your copyright. Your credits are everywhere,
your books are read, your choreography watched,

day after day, night after night. You lapse into the
parabola of a sigh, you are so air-tight, and we so blind.

43

COMFORT

She woke in a clear country, "relatively free
of gargoyles" and relativity. The greenish xylem
was paraphrase in the soft garden and the hyperspace
lazy, as if Sunday were the only day except Saturday

which would soon be Sunday and she couldn't
light a match or do a dish or make merry with any
utility or even consider a check on a list or make a list
or drive or shop, but could walk in a forest,

or walk in a park. The air was fair, almost
proverbial. A squirrel was almost a squirrel there,
but less torrential. The moss was myrrh, and old lovers
came nowhere near the mind. The path was empty

and simmering in weather reports one waits
a year for, the grass refining gradients like mercury.

SWEET DEMISE

You, so lowercased and askew, you whom
I "never seek to tell..." —all elemi without a tree,
all Amman in fecundity, in the hubbub-dub thrum
of post-thou and post-thee, wow me

belly-up, replete and insistent. There is
the simple problem of nonexistence before we
meet and after we meet, the clouded cavities between

dogberry dalliances, the unremembering veil
that inhales resurrections, reincarnations, lost mail,
and inhabits each eyelash and fingernail as we

speak, a dwelling you find more comfortable
than proximity, so, go, cling to the benumbing
inspring, the prenatal headstone with a hyphen between,
or skip the hyphen, if that's your thing; nil me.

FAINT FERVOR

Surely a memory may become unreeved,
forgotten, not the big ones just the little ones, surely
the little ones, the hairs on the top of a hand, the inexpensive
shoes, the rumpled slacks and Salvation Army satchel,

may, like a savarin containing too much rum, be sent
back with a tip, to oblivion. Surely, you will concede on this
very minor need to dispel levity for deeper rebeldoms
of more import than the redroot or pantaloon,

or whatever little memories embosom, and banish
them as junkiques from the living room where taut issues
dwell. I'm tired of keeping them, their might-as-well
intransigence. They reappear as melting popsicles

in the fridge, leaving me to mop-up, late for the cantina,
unushered to the frug, by hoodlums, as far too tender.

THRESHOLD

Summer was damaging, all the semaphore's flags
ripped off in the wind, a hurricane of white butterflies
rhapsodizing the din, gingerly matting the decimation
that left paradise empty as a gaping stage

before Balanchine moved in, or after he left,
either direction fits, the rainout endless and maundering.
Yet, you advertise absence as if you want something:
a retinue of Phooeys in the marblish green,

or galyak slippers, to keep you company,
allurances like snapdragons to pastel the solitude
that is so confusing and moody it distracts Austrian burrs
from overgrowing the path, and makes the rocket

larkspur droopy. Nothing lasts, you surprisingly say.
Agreed, agreed, but a rat-tail cactus keeps prickling me.

AUTO-AUTUMN

\What happened to sweet heat, the sneezeweed,
the luna moth and gingham sleeve, sipped Slurpies
and reedy kayaks, the sponge-bathed trees? Why
are the nights so flustered and furrowed,

dusks crimped by crooked V's of snow geese
bored with palmettos? Why does the full moon
pinprick the draft, neurotic winds re-entering therapy,
the light, an ash blonde with a melanoma scare,

suddenly draped? And why can't one escape
this surly schedule, or, like a mule chained to a wheat
thrasher, adjust to the cycle? But, oh no, optimism

is unavailable, gone crop-dusting below Mexico,
leaving the crotchety with self-help manuals on how
to let go, stay thin, be alone, and feel wonderful.

REDOLENT WILES

The red strawflower in the straw hour
is ready-made, a tiptoe in the roomful day
as the slight chill of Fall enters a window in a ratiné
shawl. The flower says: "My forgiveness,

you are a bit cold, but what a brassy caftan
you've brought home." Consummations, window-flown,
jangle the thatched redhead, a neighbor to thistles and
deadheads, a rattled rondel when alone. The wishful

titillations of brisk cool air have her clinging
to the window screen, its veiny bustle, making the vased
room a vivarium of elemental love. "My forgiveness,
what did you do in the arboretum?" she continues,

but the chilly wind is dumb, slightly frizzled,
from erasing all the thrummed places it came from.

MOCK ORANGE

Delia days—the sun as smooth as waxed legs,
the heat crimped, the leaves: flitting alliterations
of "lilygreen" in susurrant glades near waxed streams,
daydreams eerie as elflocks on an tilted manikin—

sink into winter as a sigh folded within an envelope
pressed between two volumes of Pope, then left, enclosed
by wan willows, in an abandoned kiosk; delia days, their weary
weasels and benumbed chariot steeds neither spry nor

fevered: are these whispered caesuras the emptiness
that falls between us when we creep toward dual eloignments,
in opposite directions, of course, under a waxed firmament,

so all tears, wherever they fall, only slide? And only
such surfaces can survive eiderdowns of compromise where
tears are too deep to bypass a cheek, much less arrive?

NOVEMBER MORE

Loury light, lank white and clustered, ushers
the infinitesimal doluge of musk that is autumn's fatal
touch to the coma of heat as it still breathes and broathes,
its eyes shut in moiling dreams of obese pigeons

near soused picnics as they wave wobbly farewells
to bandshelled cicadas, their audience of hyacinths and fleas.
It was a sturdy summer the low loury light now nurses
in abstract routines, one that basked in juggleries

of sate bumblebees, a bawdy sovereign to gravid
spiders, bunched in brown knots under the rungs of garden
ladders from which heaving privets were trimmed and
trimmed. Now, the old geezer is mighty slim,

the loury footfalls shuffle in, soundless swanskin
on linoleum, before a more complete whiteness begins.

OIL BIRDS

"When we build our missile defense system,
sandbars will drink kava, high winds will be polished
and peaceful, limbo will climb out of limbo, gaze at silver
flutes, and there will be no bad calls in jujitsu.

When we build, mayflies in stammering amplitudes,
will ruffle the beards of philosophers with gentle ether,
and junkets will have no travel delays, as well, because when
we build, we build for the people, people with jackdaws,

good people. And our parks, with their jollyboats
and slavers, are clean. We're tender at heart, sangfroid-steady,
our kids, too: they're sacrosanct, important as Stradivari,
in fact, to be undubious about it. Missiles matter,

down to the smallest kazoo, which is why we're proposing
to you our missile plan, a plan you'll grow accustomed to."

GLORY

After dusks in Arlington, when the hindquarters
of black horses bearing reversed saddles disappear
into crisp stables to be tended with the utmost care,
war medals, like bottle caps, pop into the air

and hover above the graves like ribboned gnats,
gone out of the dust in a nocturnal fuss to twitch there
as if the sky were a wishing well with lots of loose pennies
in it, and not one "come true" to settle them down.

The gates and parking lots, vacant as a nose
upon a skull, are closed, the remembering relatives back
at motels watching news commentators in-the-know

make reverent stern commitments, the medals
a-bobble in whirligig fits, in mini-swoons and pirouettes,
above the once-slow breathers who took the last hit.

WOMBWARD

The day was too long, the schist too beautiful,
the gold too burnished, the chivalrous too manful,
she wanted to be flung back, uterine, enfolded, neither
girl nor boy, but undetermined: a snug nub

slightly conceived, faintly sensual, hooked up
to the heart's gamelan orchestra where she could
breathe, dim and moonless, a muffle on a sonogram,
an inception of an oculus; remade as simple,

and not javelin-hurled toward the tip
of a sword to be impaled by presswork, born
to convince the inconvincible to toss off the scabbard
and get real; while, all around, in lancet noons,

lovers kiss, bodhisattvas swoop down to nuzzle
the boarfish, and accidents give kidneys to one another.

four **THE KEYHOLE GARDEN**

THE KEYHOLE GARDEN

Birds are better than words; like lungfish
on a petri dish, they have their worlds. They squawk
and finagle, their collations shrewd: packrats in the Psaltery,
they pseudo-soothe in thready cacophonies

the Wedgewood blues that drop by like palm readers
to trace the treasure map of melancholy, in case you want
to head out and never find your way back after attaining nothing
but the residue of a burglary. It is pleasure to see,

rather than explore rank territory, birds, their feathery
dysfunctional families, their feisty arguments over a dinner
of seeds. How swiftly they move on, to other traumas,

other scenes, as if attention-deficiency-syndrome needed
no therapy, but was actually liberating and flattering to trees.

FEATHER-FLOWN

There was a laughing photograph that laughed
at the photographer who laughed back until the creases
of the laugh twinned and became perfectly aligned.
Then, glassine slipped between them,

absorbing both, and became an alamode mist
of *a la monde* that floats above lazarettos and hobos,
lawn bowlers and braided vines, as a missing photograph
of the inestimable, in an inestimable amount of time.

Come back, photograph. It is too rare
that anyone laughs. Come down to the scribble
of smiles, the earth-stained chameleons and epitaphs.

Come down to the blousy cries of those
who need more muffs. Come down to the cold and
curious who think too much: to the fingertip, the touch.

EASY COMPANY

Lank lateens in winds of morphemes, these bluffs,
yet, the earth is flat, the ravines swallowed. The moosemilk
seas pull back from the spirula'd hollows that bubble
the sands to a pinweed world, a world without

shadows and fans, where morning moppets dwell
in phaetons of dawn. There, not in this sedulous vessel,
there are no rooms, there are no laws, between the quicksets
and many many walls. Do you, freefall, once

a grenadier in a hospital and still mopping-up, ever
pause to see the silvering lookdowns of shadowless ponds,
their tit-tat-toe's of tadpoles, pink salmon yet to spawn,

or are you everbound to nightshifts, afraid to leave
the army, its schemozzled schedules without mufti, and
retire, benignly, for a few minutes of sensible love?

TO A FRIEND WRITING A MEMOIR

Vast and timorous, the afternoon's elegance
shadows the ad hoc hymns of departed crickets
within green breakers of ferns. A limp wind swishes…
swishes the salty pines, those tipsy sailors.

It is cold, cold and hot. The oblivion of cities
invades the fallen spines of the mulched forest
where birds, wise in disappearance, flee. Home fires
revive lost fathers amid so-lonesome-I-could-die

cinders. Once, two men touched in salmon rivers.
Once, a headstone butterfly'd a wooden crib. All
was innocence. No brother died. Overdoses
were milk from nipples. Now, the what-

I-regret-the-most survivors, alone and childless,
elegize these all-too-cauterized deep incisions
that tattoo, with henna-stains, long slow lives.

DAYTRIPPING

She arrived all wrong, well-dressed, a bracelet
on her wrist, lapis lazuli, underwear pressing against
a long beige dress, sandals stylish and elevated. She
thought the presentation through but missed

the Simone Weilian interest in a runaway day
near the river in Cambridge where only real estate
gets away with showy opulence. She could throw
all those clothes away, she won't, she didn't,

she is neither alluring nor innocent, made
malleable not by spirit, but by mass media, subliminally,
by Vogue's preening impossibility, by Bride mag,
peripherally, by Oprah's umph and pull,

or by a fairy tale with swans wearing shirts sewn
from sea anemones, by anything ruffling or external.

SAVING MONEY

Nothing gets dust off like water and a cloth so throw
away your Mr. Clean and, in a year, attend an opera, free,
in a layaway seat, plush in the intervals of the elite,
alounge in costumed passion, exquisite sound,

as a tourist in the pique of what's always around,
but, head to the floorboards, slips by. You've earned
your keep, your assets unrecognized by your very eyes,
your room is neat, the clock a nice neighbor,

how long have you labored without *Geneviève
de Brabant*? Now, with "de rigueur" a shut-out, and schedules
more economical, you may leave the onyx-sky wallpaper
for a fracture of a scalped ticket to relax within

Offenbach's panned bacchanal, his phallic surge
immemorable, and return with a playbill, a salvaged tremble.

BEACH BALM

Spysats peep with aplomb at the hand-carved
melancholy plum, whittled, with fingernail clippers,
out of a knobbed piece of driftwood that entered the moat
of a sand castle abandoned before it was done.

Tenuous fruit, palsied as a kukui nut, odd-angled
as a kneecap upon a cadaver; an orange-tinted plastic
bowl awaits you in the techno-digs of a videographer who
films parking lots in Queens and shares strange,

troublesome dreams with his straightfaced mother
who cannot help but crack a smile when the dream's psychic
violence swizzles and she tires of the motionless pose
she's assigned to. Objet de mórbido, salt-bound

rue, precisely essential to the dead-pan video school,
plangent puce plumb; it's you we accrue, only you.

SWEVENS

Inspirited vacuums, sculpted between streaks of rain,
phantoms who bathe Lazarus in Miriams of mists—riddle
the downpour's pixilated grays. They seem to come;
they seem to move away: wavering silhouettes

in the plashed silence. Do they see you? Or is it
you who see them turn and bend, as caryatids of water,
toward moist shielings, water pastures, to lend a herdsman
a brimming bowl? Or do they roll into rivulets

toward quays, rushing away decay below thunder?
Will they reappear in a temple where momentum is prayer
and will they stay there? Or are they veiled changelings

wombed in the glaze of heavy rain that encloses
them, as if they, too, are bathed and risen from the dead, and
blessed in the pale, vanquishing addendum?

SPRINGWOOD ESPOUSAL

In fairy-flanged environs, the scale of justice
is puddle-hopped by a frog prince, balancing two brass
pans between weight and absence in a horizontal shimmer
of swift symmetry, as Io—no, Syrinx—no, Demeter—

God, no—as a Thracian maid too slow to nip Orpheus
watches the prince from a grassy divan, nonplussed by
undulating stratagems that pop up from everywhere
like Zeus foreheads lurking amid delphiniums.

"One day, you'll tip that scale," she breathes
fluent in the damask shale. "I won't, I won't, I won't,"
the green regent responds, his rhythmic swiveling hops,
brawny. "You will, too," she continues, lulled by

the unconflicted blur of side-long thighs, "a windsock
in eternity floats down to tip all bongo-board rides."

RIP RAP

Harbors of cavalla and cradled lagoons, honed
satinwood drifting ashore, enamelling an upside-down moon,
the pirate-winds laggard in the spirit compass as if dropped
from a purse: it is here we turn in turnaways, return,

and converse, sweet excretias of sweat moistening
the verve; and, you suggest, in this gull-swept wantoness
of inhaled blues, that there is no other on the beach to wave
to? No footfall on the sperrylite sands? No you?

That all rolls in lachrymose strolls toward tombs,
tombs without room for two? Ah, even the hawk moths serve
from this platitude and rise above the tide, the liquid

multi-moon's specious light. They know their meridians,
their bridal flights, the catch-all cushions of beached nights.
Swiveling, they disappear, leaving the starlessness lazy.

MESA MISCHIEF

The iron trestles break, like spiderwebs a gardener
shakes while plucking a yellow leaf off a quiet rhododendron
to tuckpoint the evergreen. Vertumnus would be pleased,
but Hurricane Bob has arrived in a Trollope-novel

of rain, dropkicking thundercaps over goalposts
of manic oaks, smashing hedges as if they'd just grabbed
a fumble. Connections lapse in the mishmash sylviculture.
Trundel beds of mums disappear. It is Tuesday, it is

Sunday. Normandy is a town in Missouri, the ocean's
swink a tiny stream, a truepenny. Pan, in baffled shambles,
has lost his pipe in "a teardrop of a lake" in southeast
Nevada. We could lasso the tawny fray, listen to

Lost-and-found tunes with an Olympian castaway, before
the Recreational Vehicles break camp, and we awake to today.

RIGHT ON

Death is such an interesting topic. Really. The trees
are alounge, hoping you will speak even more about it
than you already have, what with knuckles clenched
in a necro-caress under the breezeless spiras,

the world above a misdo of spin-offs,
of suffocating assumptions plagued by pain,
embittering the wattles. And how nice it is, enwrapped in
damp sphagnum, to be removed from the monkeyshine,

its caveats and encomiums, to rest in the quiet
irrefutable dark, orlopped among the paca, in a murex vacuum
that shuns tippets of rumination for lidded certitude,

overindulgences beguiled. The tiger-beetles
are too-too: Toscanini was right. All that remains is
a vandal, tugging the lost spermary into twilight.

BIRDBATH

Days of bluejays, days of the sundial,
when journalism fades into epigrams of a child:
the outline of a cockatoo in a highfalutin cloud,
witches at the doorknob in black nightgowns.

A garden reencircles the earth's iced rims
with coloringbook camel trails and Rin-Tin-Tin.
A feather falls to jelloed lawns, a mud wasp withers,
someone in an apron calls with a warmed-up dinner.

A nice breeze swivvers, an elementary bray—
all the boys will go to Nam and all the girls will stay
and when the boys come home again, fat fronds will sway,
the garden like a paradigm that never went away.

Days of bluejays, days of the sundial,
how nearly actual your lost, entrancing smile.

LAYING LOW

The dandelions on Summer Street
in an over-familiar town, lift to an inviolate lake
undistracted by the clapboarded ground.

There, a chubby boy with a removable neck tatoo
offers up a blueberry, above a black poodle.

If evil's ever absent, lost in an annal,
behind a July of butterflies
above a rubber sandal,

let it be
gone from the sand
at an unfashionable lakefront
above a boy's open hand.

"THERE IS ONLY SUN, SUNSTRIFE AND SEA"

Your home is unmonikered, lost as a valise
left on a train at a stop between the arrows of weathervanes.
No cola nuts, no logos, mark the domain where

loving grows. It is a filament beaded by spiderlings,
juju enjambments, or flivvery pings, ablauts in a tinted
vitrine, an interstice, an interpass, amid coveralls of houses
surrounded by speedwells in the cool smatter-dash.

Does it last, does it matter? Do the zinc toned
passenger pigeons descend, out of the swallowing
ozone, to remail a letter? Or will the brooks dissolve them
once again in the slow leeward agenda? Who can

say where home is, letterbound or letter-sent, or where
the pigeons came from or where the pigeons went.

ABOUT THE POET

Star Black is the author of four books of poetry: *Double Time*, *Waterworn*, *October for Idas*, and *Balefire*. She is also co-founder of the long-running poetry reading series at the KGB Bar in Manhattan's East Village, and teaches writing at the New School University.

Born in Coronado, California, and raised in Washington D.C. and in Hawaii, Black attended Wellesley College before spending six years in Southeast Asia, where she wrote travel books and taught English to Thai college students. She moved to New York after joining United Press International as a staff photographer. Black remained a Midtown resident after leaving UPI, earned an MFA degree from Brooklyn College, and pursued a freelance career as a photographer and visual artist. Her photographs have appeared on the cover of *Newsweek* and in *The New York Times*, and her drawings and collages have been shown at numerous galleries in New York.

The NEW YORK POETS SERIES *celebrates the strength and sweep of New York City's poetry community. It features the work of poets long-admired in New York and beyond for their development of a distinctive idiom and a unique poetic identity.*